555 Sticker Fun Horses and Unicorns

Written by Oakley Graham
Illustrated by Bradley Hunt and Lauren Ellis

TOP THAT

Licensed exclusively to Top That Publishing Ltd
Tide Mill Way, Woodbridge, Suffolk, IP12 1AP, UK
www.topthatpublishing.com

0 2 4 6 8 9 7 5 3 1
Manufactured in China

The Enchanted Forest

Welcome to the Enchanted Forest, a place where horses and unicorns come to meet and play. Add more horses and their magical unicorn friends to the happy scene.

Over the rainbow

Horses and unicorns must cross the Magical Rainbow Bridge to reach the Enchanted Forest. The bridge is made with special fairy magic! Add fluttering fairy friends to the scene.

Forest friends

Unicorns are not the only magical creatures that live and play in the Enchanted Forest. Find some more amazing forest friends and add them to the scene.

Magical candy copse

Horses and unicorns love minty sweet treats! They cannot believe their eyes when they discover a copse of candy delights in the Enchanted Forest. Add more treats for the friends to munch.

Moonlit pony parade

Every year there is a fabulous pony parade through the Enchanted Forest. Add more little ponies and twinkling lights to the magical moonlit procession.

At the races

Horses and unicorns love to gallop and they really enjoy racing against their friends! Who will win this race around the Enchanted Forest track?

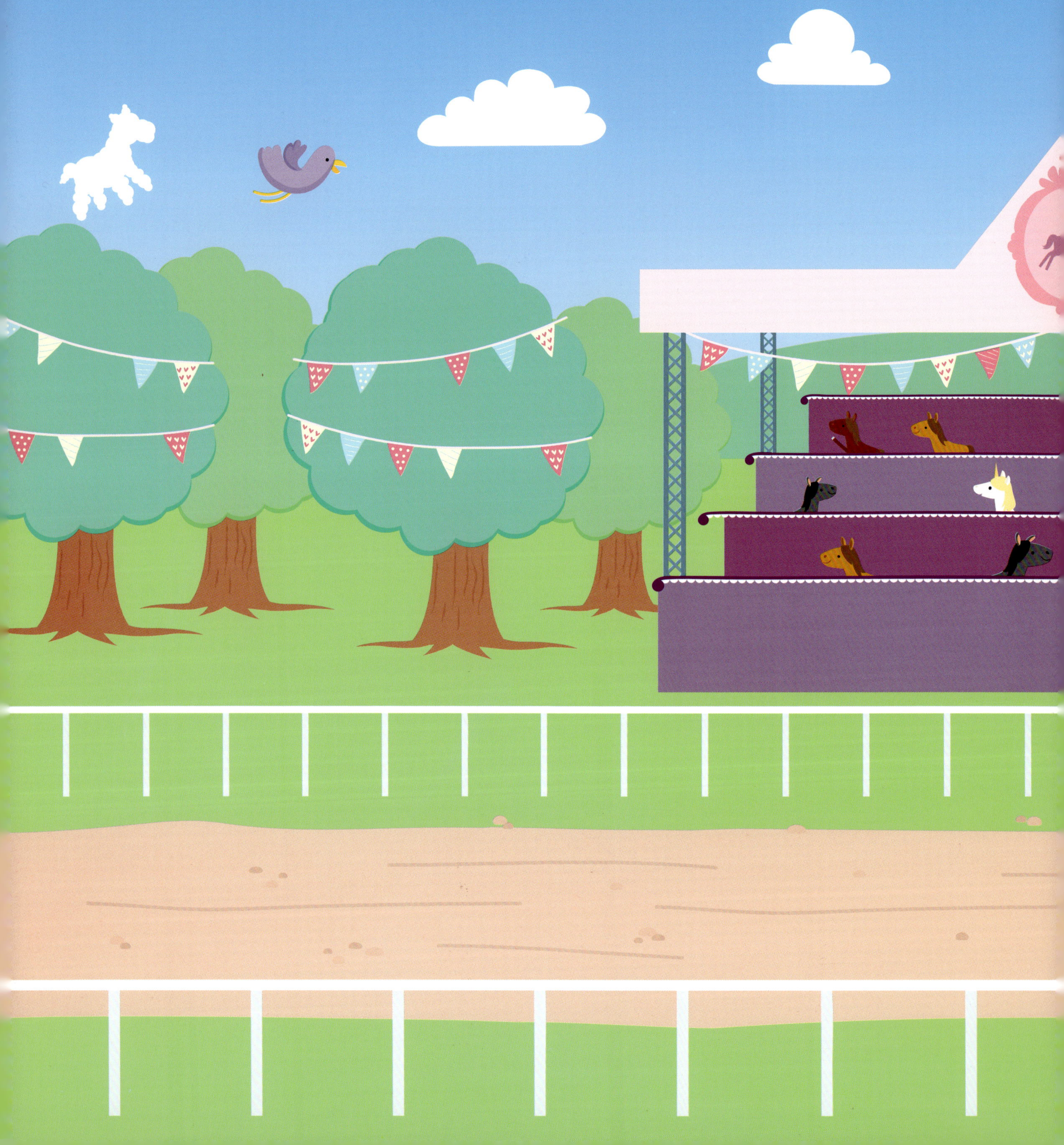

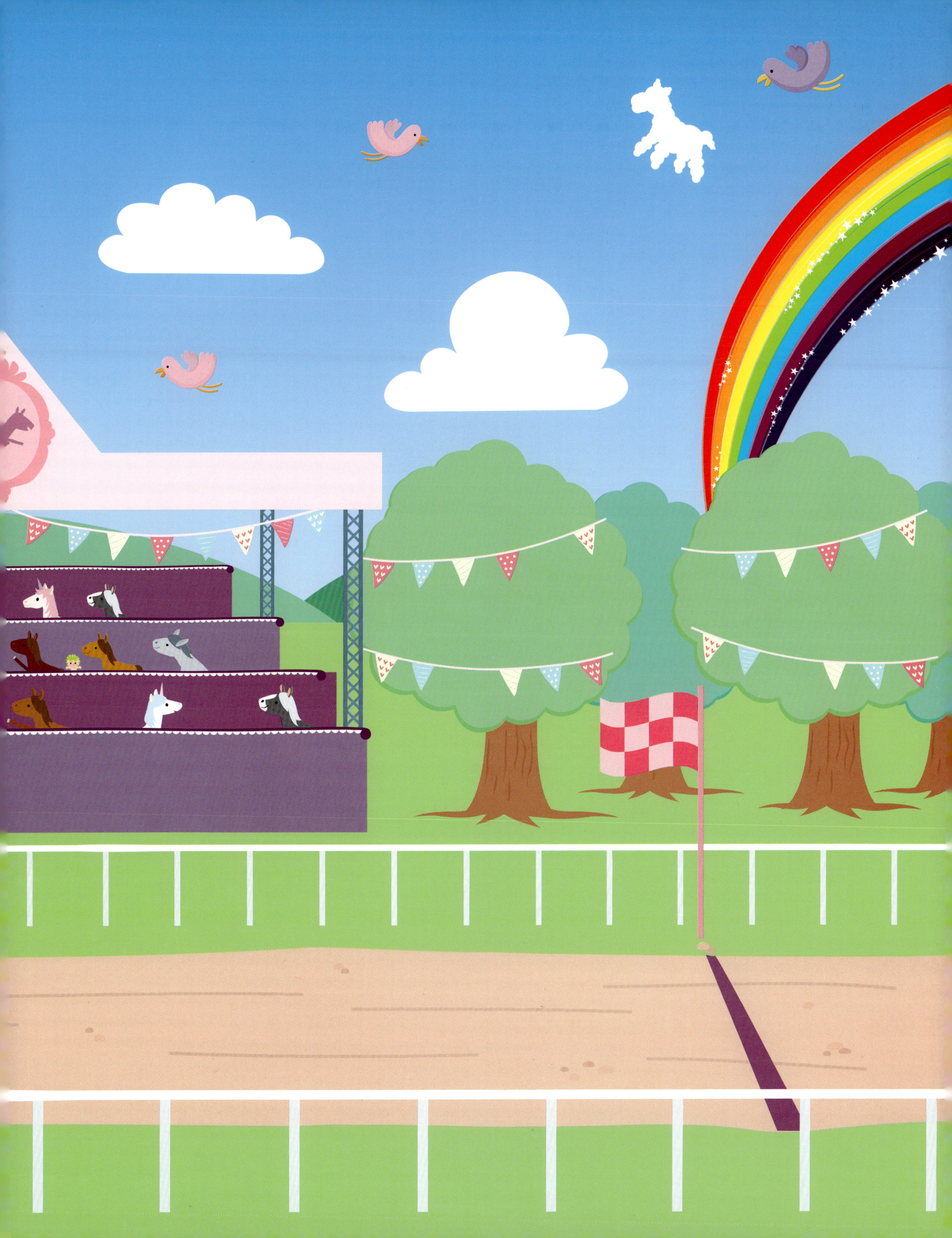

Midsummer ball

On the longest day of the year, the unicorns hold a magnificent midsummer ball. Manes are coloured and hooves are painted for this most magical of celebrations.

Cute creatures

Unicorns help to protect the other animals who live in the Enchanted Forest. Find some more forest animals to complete the best friends scene.

Winter wonderland

It's a magical moonlit night, and the horses and unicorns are playing in a snowy glade. Add more fantastic beasts to the wintry scene.

Fable stables

After a long day galloping around the Enchanted Forest, the horses like to relax in their stables. Help the fairies to give them buckets of food and some blankets to keep them warm.

Troll time

Unicorns won't let anyone or anything ride them, apart from trolls! Add more of these colourful little characters to the scene.

Wild berry harvest

Horses and unicorns love eating wild berries and the Enchanted Forest is full of them! Add more for the happy horses, unicorns and fairies to collect to make a feast.

Unicorn trials (dressage)

It's the day of the riderless dressage championship and unicorns from all over the Enchanted Forest have come to compete. Add unicorns performing skilful manoeuvres to the stadium scene.

Unicorn trials (cross-country)

Cross-country trials are tough and there are lots of tricky obstacles for the unicorns to jump over. Add more obstacles and unicorns to the course.

Unicorn trials (showjumping)

It's the final event of the unicorn trials and the contestants are neck and neck! Who will win the showjumping event and be crowned the champion this year?

Motherly love

Some of the unicorns have just given birth to their very first foal! Add more foals next to their proud mothers in this springtime scene.

Pegasus

Pegasus is the only winged horse in the Enchanted Forest. He loves to swoop in and out of the clouds playing tag with his hippogriff friends.

Hide-and-seek

Horses and unicorns love to play hide-and-seek! Hide more horse and unicorn friends so they are difficult to spot in amongst the trees.

Magical maze

Some parts of the Enchanted Forest are just like a maze! Fill the forest with horses and unicorns trying to reach the special prize in the middle.

Mountain picnic

Tall mountains rise up in the centre of the Enchanted Forest. Close to the tallest peak, there is a perfect place for horses and unicorns to enjoy a picnic! Make the amazing view even better.

Mermaid lake

Mermaids talk to the horses and unicorns as they stop to drink water at Mystic Lake. Seahorses pop up to say hello to their four-legged friends, too. Finish the happy, chatty scene.

Night-Mare!

Not all of the horses and unicorns who live in the Enchanted Forest are good. Everyone is scared of Night-Mare and his naughty friends. Make the scene more friendly with a moon, stars, lanterns and fireflies.

A unicorn wedding

These unicorns are madly in love and they're getting married! Finish off the happy scene so the couple can celebrate in style!

Good neigh-bours!

Horses and unicorns love to be groomed! Their good fairy neighbours always keep their manes and tails tangle-free! Add fairies with grooming items to the scene.